Lord of our world

Lord of our world

Modern collects from the gospels

Susan Williams

 Falcon · London

First Published 1973
© Copyright Susan Williams 1973
ISBN 0 85491 559 1

FALCON BOOK
published by Church Pastoral Aid Society,
Falcon Court, 32 Fleet Street, London EC4Y 1DB

Overseas Agents
EMU Book Agencies Ltd, 1 Lee Street,
Sydney, NSW, Australia
Scripture Union, 177 Manchester Street,
Christchurch, New Zealand
Sunday School Centre Wholesale, PO Box 3020,
Cape Town, South Africa
Anglican Book Society, 228 Bank Street,
Ottawa K2P 1X1, Canada

Made and printed in Great Britain by
Hunt Barnard Printing Ltd., Aylesbury, Bucks.

Contents

Foreword

This book of collects fills a long-felt need. Susan Williams is not competing with Cranmer – who could hope to do so? – but providing an alternative to him in the context of the revised liturgical services. Cranmer's great gift to the Church was his pithy, cool, objective style which has survived centuries of change and remans still a model for his successors. Cranmer's style is reflected in the brevity and directness of the collects in this book, but the subject matter reflects the much wider range of interest in the Church today and permits a greater variety of feeling and response in the mind of the individual worshipper. They have the virtue also of linking directly with the gospel for the day and thus enabling the service in Church or prayers in the home to be gathered round a single, dominant theme. They are short enough to be remembered easily and to be worked into a daily pattern of prayer and recollection. Susan Williams is to be congratulated on maintaining so high a standard throughout what must have been an extremely arduous exercise in composition.

STUART LIVERPOOL.

Introduction

Prayer is an activity which goes beyond words, and beyond thought itself. But at some stage words are needed, and hence written prayers. The prayers in this collection are short. Most are single sentences. In fact they are collects; an ancient form ideally suited to modern language and needs. The best twentieth century furniture has clean simple lines, shorn of the kind of beauty which collects dust. The best modern language is the same; alive and beautiful, rhythmic and simple. This is the ideal. I point to it rather than approach it, but the aim is there.

Prayer springs from the Gospels. The life-time experience of the men who knew Christ breathes His life into ours. We know Him; we know Him through the Holy Spirit; we know Him in the Gospels and in ourselves. He shapes our thoughts and prayers.

In this book I have taken the Gospel passages set in the new Series 3 lectionary of the Anglican Church and written two collects for each Sunday in the two-year cycle, and one for each saint's day. Some are repeated where a particular passage or theme is repeated. And an indexed supplement indicates collects for use with the Gospels of the 1662 lectionary. The quotation printed before each prayers is a reminder of the whole passage rather than a statement of the exact subject of the prayer. Sometimes a theme is so embedded in the text that no few words isolated from it can make an adequate introduction. The prayers for saint's days sometimes have very little to do with their particular saint, this is because they are based on the passage rather than the occasion. For a similar reason the themes of the prayers do not always correspond with the titles given to each Sunday in the proposed New Calendar. These titles are drawn from the 'controlling lesson' which, at certain times of the year, is the Epistle or the Old Testament reading, and not the Gospel.

This is the framework of the book, but the prayers are not, I hope, tied rigidly to it, and can stand on their own apart from the passages which inspired them.

I have written with the following people in mind: those who conduct prayers in Church and at meetings; those who give talks and sermons based on the Gospel for the day; and those who read and pray privately at home.

I should like to thank three people: my husband, for encouraging me to write; Canon C. B. Naylor, for reading the manuscript and offering valuable advice and suggestions; and the Bishop of Liverpool, for his kindness in writing a foreword and for reading and commenting on the manuscript.

SUSAN WILLIAMS

Sundays
and Major Festivals
first year

1   ' . . . *the celestial powers will be shaken. And then*
        they will see the Son of Man coming on a
        cloud . . . '
        Lord, who will come again as surely as summer
        follows spring, keep us steady when the world
        reels about us, and make us ready for the coming
        of Your kingdom with great power and glory:
        Amen.

2   ' . . . *when you see all this happening, you may*
        know that the kingdom of God is near . . . '
        Father God, Your promises buried in the dust of
        time came gloriously alive in Christ; keep us
        faithful to You for all time, that in Your
        kingdom we may join the great family which
        praises You with a single voice: Amen.

JOHN 5.36–47   Second Sunday in Advent

3   '*There is enough to testify that the Father has sent*
        me, in the works my Father gave me to do . . . '
        Lord Jesus, Your works were charged with the
        energy of God; recharge our faith: Lord Jesus,
        Your works were left for us to finish; renew our
        strength; and bring the Father's glory into our
        lives and into the world: Amen.

4   '*You study the scriptures diligently, supposing that*
    in having them you have eternal life . . . '
    Lord God, whose Son confounded the Bible
    experts of His day, confound the darkness in our
    minds and send us light, that in reading Your
    Word we may see our Lord, and seeing, may
    believe: Amen.

JOHN 1.19–27   Third Sunday in Advent

5   '*This is the testimony which John gave . . . He*
    confessed without reserve . . . '
    Lord God, You loved the world and made us
    Your messengers and sons; take from us our
    timidity, and give us grace to declare You boldly
    to all who ask our business, for the sake of the
    Son who died for all and gave us our commission:
    Amen.

6   '*I am a voice crying aloud in the wilderness . . .* '
    God of the impossible, who sent John to shout
    in a desert and people came to hear, send us into
    the desert areas of modern life with the boldness
    of John and the message of the coming of Your
    Son: Amen.

7   ' *"How can this be?" said Mary . . .* '
     All-demanding loving Father, You call us to
     work beyond our human powers; send us Your
     command and the gift of Your Holy Spirit, that
     our lives may bring in Your promises and declare
     the greatness of our Lord: Amen.

8   '*I am the Lord's servant; as you have spoken, so
     be it.*'
     God of the impossible, whose angel spoke of
     Isaac's birth and Sarah laughed; give to us the
     mind of Mary, who heard a greater promise and
     believed, that as Your Spirit speaks in our hearts,
     so it may be in our lives, through Jesus Christ
     our Lord, obedient to death and King for ever:
     Amen.

     *Also to be found at The Annunciation of the Blessed Virgin
     Mary (250)*

9   '*She . . . laid him in a manger, because there was
     no room for them to lodge in the house.*'
     Lord, You were born in an overcrowded city;
     come to our overcrowded lives: Lord, You fill the
     universe; fill the inner world of our minds, that
     we may know one thing, Your forgiving love,
     and do one thing, lay our lives at Your feet:
     Amen.

10   ' . . . the shepherds returned glorifying and praising
     God for what they had heard and seen . . . '
     Lord Jesus Christ, born coloured and poor,
     welcomed by working men and kings, come to
     our world and heal our deep divisions, that we
     may be not white and black, male and female,
     employer and employed, but the children of God,
     seeing You, our Lord, in one another: Amen.

MATTHEW 2.1–12   First Sunday after Christmas

11   'We observed the rising of his star, and we have
     come to pay him homage.'
     Lord Jesus, worshipped by foreigners who read
     the signs of the times and recognized a king,
     teach us to read the signs of our own times
     which mark Your presence in this world, and lead
     us to live our lives in obedience to Your kingly
     rule: Amen.

     *Also to be found at First Sunday after Christmas, second
     year (133)*

12   ' . . . then they opened their treasures and offered
     him gifts . . . '
     Lord Jesus, You received gifts from strangers;
     help us who are adopted into God's family to
     obey You as king, to worship You as Lord, to
     share in Your death and to rejoice with You in
     your resurrection: Amen.

     *Also to be found at First Sunday after Christmas, second
     year (134)*

13   ' . . . *he came into the temple; and when the*
      parents brought in the child Jesus . . . he took him
      in his arms . . . '
      Lord God, You kept faith with Simeon and
      showed him the infant king; give us grace to put
      all our trust in Your promises, and the patience
      to wait a lifetime for their fulfilment, through
      Jesus Christ our Lord, on whom faith depends
      from start to finish: Amen.

      Also to be found at The Presentation of Christ in the
      Temple (248)

14   '*She never left the temple, but worshipped day and*
      night, fasting and praying.'
      Lord God, faithful for ever, keep us faithful to
      You a day at a time; teach us to pray today and
      to live in Your presence today, that at the end of
      time we may see Your Son come again in glory:
      Amen.

MATTHEW 3.13–17   First Sunday after Epiphany

15   '*Then Jesus . . . came to John to be baptized by*
      him.'
      Lord God, help us who have dipped a foot into
      the waters of life to plunge in over our heads,
      dead to the old ways and fully alive to the new,
      for the sake of Jesus, who gave His life for those
      He loved: Amen.

16   '*Then Jesus . . . came to John to be baptized by
      him. John tried to dissuade him . . .*'
      Lord, give us grace to know that our knowledge
      of You is partial, and give us the mind of John
      the Baptist, who fully obeyed Your command
      where he did not fully understand: Amen.

MARK 1.14-20   Second Sunday after Epiphany

17   '*Jesus came into Galilee proclaiming the Gospel of
      God . . .*'
      Lord Jesus, the Good News who came in person,
      we offer You our lives, to be possessed by the
      love and power which burst into Galilee, that the
      Good News of God may come to us and to our
      neighbours: Amen.

18   '*And at once they left their nets and followed
      him . . .*'
      Lord God, who sees us busy with our own affairs,
      break into our lives with Your disturbing call,
      and show us what things to abandon and what
      new things to do, for the sake of Him who is
      worth the loss of all things: Amen.

      Also to be found at St Andrew the Apostle (268)

19   *'Jesus's mother said to him, "They have no wine
      left".'*
      Lord God, You have given us a world of natural
      resources which fail and run out; renew in us
      Your other gift, Christ Himself, the one resource
      who never fails, the one power in our lives whose
      product is joy for ever: Amen.

20   *'Jesus said to the servants, "Fill the jars with
      water", and they filled them to the brim.'*
      Lord Jesus, who turned water into wine, help us
      to obey You in the details of our lives; take the
      ordinary things we do for other people and use
      them to bring the joy of Your presence into their
      lives and into the world: Amen.

MARK 2.13–17   Fourth Sunday after Epiphany

21   *' . . . he saw Levi son of Alphaeus at his seat in the
      customhouse, and said to him, "Follow me" . . . '*
      Lord God, whose Son called Matthew on a
      working day to follow Him, send us Your grace,
      that we may see and hear our Lord in our
      weekday lives, and count everything loss for the
      sake of knowing Him: Amen.

      Also to be found at St Matthew the Apostle (263)

22   *'When Jesus was at table in his house, many bad*
        characters . . . were seated with him and his
        disciples . . . '
        Lord and Father, Your Son attracted the greedy,
        the bent and the rejected, who rejoiced in His
        company; may we who enjoy His presence now
        go where He would go, for His sake and with the
        confidence of love: Amen.

MARK 2.18–22   Fifth Sunday after Epiphany

23   *'As long as they have the bridegroom with them,*
        there can be no fasting.'
        God of the depressed and anxious, pierce the
        outer skin of cheerfulness which masks our
        secret fears, and fill our inner being with Your
        joy, the joy of resurrection and of living with our
        Lord: Amen.

        Also to be found at Twenty second Sunday after Trinity,
        second year (233)

24   *'No one sews a patch of unshrunk cloth on to an*
        old coat.'
        Lord of new beginnings, save us from patching
        up our polluted world and continuing in selfish
        greed, but make us new people, fit for a new
        heaven and a new earth, through Jesus Christ our
        Lord, the beginning and end of all things: Amen.

        Also to be found at Twenty second Sunday after Trinity,
        second year (234)

25 ' . . . *the Son of Man is sovereign even over the
   Sabbath.*'
   Lord, keep our lives simple in a complex world,
   and help us to live by the single rule of love, that
   all the universe may be reunited with its Maker:
   Amen.

   *Also to be found at Trinity Sunday, second year (189) and
   Twenty first Sunday after Trinity, second year (231)*

26 '*There was a man in the congregation who had a
   withered arm . . .* '
   Lord, Your love shines in a loveless world; shine
   on us, Your weak and disabled followers, that we
   may be strong to love as You have loved us, and
   heal the world at the cost of our lives, for Your
   sake: Amen.

   *Also to be found at Twenty first Sunday after Trinity,
   second year (232)*

MATTHEW 5.1–12   **Septuagesima**

27 '*And this is the teaching he gave . . .* '
   Lord, who spoke with power, help us to meditate,
   to set Your words free in the deepest places of
   our minds, that Your strength may free us from
   our weakness, and our lives be full of joy and the
   power to do Your work: Amen.

28   '*How blest are those who know their need of God;
the kingdom of Heaven is theirs.*'
Holy Spirit, Lord of our lives, bring us to know
You in our whole being, in what we are and in
what we do; bring us the power to be the
children of God, and to do the work of God, in
the kingdom of the Son, our Lord and brother:
Amen.

*Also to be found at First Sunday after Epiphany, second
year (137)*

MARK 2.1–12   Sexagesima

29   ' . . . *a man was brought who was paralysed. Four
men were carrying him . . .* '
Lord, help us to pray for one another, the happy
for the sad, the strong for the weak, the winners
for the losers; that in Your presence we may be
forgiven, and through Your power made whole,
one body praising You for ever: Amen.

30   '*I say to you, stand up, take your bed, and go
home.*'
God of peace and of our troubled consciences,
help us to throw away past sins and present
comforts, that all our strength may be released
for the work Your Son has left for us to finish,
in His name, the Prince of Peace: Amen.

31   *'There is a boy here who has five barley loaves and
      two fishes, but what is that among so many?'*
      Lord, who used the gift of one to fill the need of
      thousands, help us so to care for others that
      without shame or despair we may offer You all
      we have, to the glory of Your name: Amen.

32   *'Then Jesus took the loaves, gave thanks and
      distributed them to the people . . . '*
      Lord, You healed the sick and fed the healthy;
      You know and meet all our needs; keep us from
      following You merely for the joy and strength
      You offer, and help us in love to take the way of
      the Cross: Amen.

      *Also to be found at Twenty sixth Sunday after Trinity,
      first year (119)*

MATTHEW 6.16–21   Ash Wednesday

33   ' *. . . and your Father who sees what is secret will
      give you your reward.'*
      Lord Jesus Christ, when the time was right You
      fasted alone in the desert; give us such hunger
      and thirst for You that we may willingly fast and
      pray in secret, and see Your power come on
      earth, and Your will done: Amen.

34   '*Do not store up for yourselves treasure on
      earth . . .*'
      Lord, who came not to raise our standard of
      living, but to bring us life abundant, help us to
      live entirely for Your kingdom, which is love, joy
      and justice, on earth and in heaven: Amen.

MATTHEW 4.1–17   First Sunday in Lent

35   '*Jesus was then led away by the Spirit into the
      wilderness, to be tempted by the devil.*'
      Lord, You were tested with a choice of three
      ways to do Your work; help us in our own lives
      always to choose the fourth way, the way of
      self-giving and of the Cross: Amen.

      Also to be found at First Sunday in Lent, second year (157)

36   '*From that day Jesus began to proclaim the
      message; "Repent, for the kingdom of Heaven is
      upon you".*'
      Lord, You have sent us into the world to make
      followers from every nation; keep us from
      offering the hungry nothing but bread, from
      presenting proofs instead of a Person, and from
      serving the forces of this world in the hope that
      they will serve us, Your messengers: Amen.

      Also to be found at First Sunday in Lent, second year (158)

37   *'When an unclean spirit comes out of a man it
      wanders over the deserts seeking a resting
      place . . .'*
      Lord, Your love has brought us to know You
      and Your power drives evil from our minds; help
      us to fill our lives with doing Your will, that Your
      presence may reach the depth of our being now
      and for ever: Amen.

38   *'If it is by the finger of God that I drive out the
      devils, then be sure that the kingdom of God has
      already come upon you.'*
      Lord, whose power to heal was tested against the
      power which destroys, and proved stronger; open
      our eyes to the signs of Your strength in this
      modern world, and open our hearts to the
      kingdom of God, which has come upon us:
      Amen.

MATTHEW 16.13–28   Third Sunday in Lent

39   *' "And you", he asked, "who do you say I am?".
      Simon Peter answered: " You are the Messiah, the
      Son of the living God".'*
      Lord of truth, teach us to live each moment
      recognizing You as king, so that everywhere we
      go our words and our working lives make plain
      the king who died in love and rose in power, to
      bring us to God: Amen.

      Also to be found at Third Sunday in Lent, second year (161)

40 '*If anyone wishes to be a follower of mine, he must leave self behind; he must take up his cross and come with me.*'
Lord Jesus Christ, who died for us, open the inward ear of our minds to hear Your voice speaking of the Cross, that we who come after You may travel with You and die daily in Your service: Amen.

Also to be found at Fourteenth Sunday after Trinity, second year (217)

MATTHEW 17.1–13   Fourth Sunday in Lent

41 ' . . . *and in their presence he was transfigured.*'
Living Lord, who links us with eternity, grant us the vision which passes in a flash but lasts for ever, and grant us all our lives to follow You: Amen.

Also to be found at Fourth Sunday in Lent, second year (163), and The Transfiguration of our Lord (259)

42 ' . . . *his face shone like the sun . . .* '
Loving Father, in our suffering send us strength; show us the glory at the heart of pain, the glory of Christ, the sufferer who died in love, that we who are freed by His death may freely love Him through death to resurrection: Amen.

Also to be found at Fourth Sunday in Lent, second year (164)

43   ' . . . *a grain of wheat remains a solitary grain*
       unless it falls into the ground and dies.'
       Lord, break our shell of self-concern and free the
       life within us struggling to expand, life which
       spreads life to others, life eternal shared with
       You, our Saviour: Amen.

44   '*And I shall draw all men to myself, when I am*
       lifted up from the earth.'
       Father God, You lifted Your Son on the Cross
       above all history and raised Him from the dead;
       draw us into His timeless presence, draw us to
       love Him, to leave the sin He has conquered, and
       to live for Him now and for ever: Amen.

       Also to be found at Twenty fourth Sunday after Trinity,
       first year (115)

MATTHEW 21.1–11   Palm Sunday

45   '*They were now nearing Jerusalem . . .* '
       Lord, You rode straight into the power of the
       enemy to suffer and die; give us the strength to
       follow You to the centres of opposition in this
       world, and the confidence which confronts power
       with love: Amen.

       Also to be found at Palm Sunday, second year (167), and
       Twenty fifth Sunday after Trinity, second year (239)

46 *'They were now nearing Jerusalem . . . '*
Lord Jesus, King of peace who led a
demonstration, lead us where true peace lies, not
in devotion to law and order, but in taking the
way of the Cross: Amen.

JOHN 19.1–37   Good Friday

47 *'Then time after time they came up to him,
crying, "Hail, King of the Jews!", and struck him
on the face.'*
Lord of every power in the universe, who did not
resist death on the Cross, give us such trust in
Your victory that we may meet all who choose
evil with non-violent love: Amen.

Also to be found at Good Friday, second year (169)

48 *' . . . he said, "It is accomplished!". He bowed his
head and gave up his spirit.'*
All-loving God, whose Son died to free us from
the grip of evil, keep us alive and free in His
kingdom, dead to self and abundantly alive to
our Lord and King, who rules for ever: Amen.

Also to be found at Good Friday, second year (170)

49   '... *they came to the tomb.*'
Lord and Father, send Your Spirit into Your
worldwide Church, that those who approach it in
sadness and despair may find the gloriously
living body of Christ, and all men may believe:
Amen.

Also to be found at Easter Day, second year (171)

50   '*He has been raised again; he is not here* ...'
Lord God, You freed Christ from death once for
all time; free us each day from our old self, that
we may live the new life of Christ now and for
ever: Amen.

Also to be found at Easter Day, second year (172)

JOHN 20.19–29   First Sunday after Easter

51   '·... *the disciples were together behind locked
doors, for fear of the Jews* ...*'
Lord Jesus Christ, we close our minds against a
threatening world because we are afraid; cross
our barricades and enter our lives, that we may
know Your peace and go out to bring it to
others: Amen.

52   *'As the Father sent me, so I send you.'*
Lord Jesus, You died for us and found Your
peace in doing the Father's will; give us the
strength to go into all the world ready to receive
wounds such as Yours, that others may know
Your peace and Your salvation: Amen.

LUKE 24.13–35   Second Sunday after Easter

53   *'Jesus himself came up and walked along with
them.'*
Lord, when we walk away from our problems,
meet us on the road; when we are defeated and
alone, bring us the joy of Your companionship,
that we may carry the power of resurrection into
a dead and despairing world: Amen.

54   *'He had been recognized by them at the breaking
of the bread.'*
Lord, Your followers recognized You in the
breaking of bread; grant us the same power that
we may know the same joy, and grant us the
same unity that we may spread the same faith:
Amen.

55   *'He said, "Shoot the net to starboard, and you will make a catch." They did so . . . '*
Risen Lord, in all things alone supreme, show us Your will and help us to obey, that in daily obedience we may discover Your presence, and Your primacy over all created things: Amen.

56   *'Then the disciple whom Jesus loved said to Peter, "It is the Lord!" '*
God of life and truth, help us to grasp the evidence of those who saw and heard and touched our risen Lord, and help us like them to follow Him to death: Amen.

57   *' . . . do you love me more than all else? . . . Then feed my lambs . . . '*
Lord of love, You gave Your life for Your sheep; send us leaders who have given their lives to You, that they may be filled with love for You alone, and we may be fed the words of eternal life, and be one flock, following You for ever: Amen.

58   *'Feed my sheep.'*
Lord, You feed us daily with the words of life;
help us daily to grow in love for You until we
freely share with all Your family the endless
resources of Your boundless love: Amen.

JOHN 16.25–33   Fifth Sunday after Easter

59   *'Do you now believe? Look, the hour is coming . . .*
when you are all to be scattered . . . leaving me
alone.'
Father, Son, and Spirit, Lord of all that is whole,
heal the divisions in our personalities; join our
doing with our thinking, our feeling with
believing, that we may be whole as You are
whole, and, living in your presence, find in You
our peace: Amen.

60   *'In the world you will have trouble. But courage!*
The victory is mine . . . '
Lord God, whose Son took on Himself the
miseries and hatreds of all people; help us to
move out from our defensive walls and live
exposed to a dangerous world, in company with
Him who conquered it: Amen.

61   *'Go forth therefore . . . '*
Lord God, send Your love into our hearts, that
we may gladly go into the world which Christ has
left and spread the good news of His kingdom in
the power which He has given us: Amen.

Also to be found at Ascension Day, second year (183)

62   *' . . . make all nations my disciples.'*
Father God, as there is one Christ in heaven,
make us one body on earth, that we may do the
will of our Lord and Head in the joy of unity,
and make Him known throughout the world:
Amen.

Also to be found at Ascension Day, second year (184)

LUKE 24.44–53   **Sunday after Ascension Day**

63   *' . . . until you are armed with the power from
above.'*
Lord God, You send us out to spread good news,
and we are hindered by our inner enemies, fear,
selfishness, uncertainty; Lord Christ, forgive, arm
us with Your power, conquer these contradictions
of Your love, and make us fit to bring Your
news to others: Amen.

*Also to be found at Sunday after Ascension Day, second
year (186)*

64 '. . . until you are armed with the power from above.'
Lord God, You brought the universe into a unity
in Christ, and this is the measure of Your power;
unite Your people on earth with Your Son in
heaven, that in Your power we may bring Him
to all people: Amen.

*Also to be found at Sunday after Ascension Day, second
year (185)*

JOHN 14.15–27   Whit Sunday

65 '. . . the Holy Spirit . . . will teach you everything,
and will call to mind all that I have told you.'
Lord of a technical age where knowledge is stored
in computers and human minds are left blank,
restore our will to learn and send us Your Spirit,
that all the words of Your Son may be printed
on our hearts and in our lives: Amen.

Also to be found at Whit Sunday, second year (187)

66 'Peace is my parting gift to you . . . '
God of an explosive world, where bombs and
weapons talk, send into our hearts the dynamite
of Your Spirit, that we may know power and
peace together, and speak of You to all people in
ways which reach the centre of their being: Amen.

Also to be found at Whit Sunday, second year (188)

67   '*Lord, show us the Father . . .*'
       God of all knowledge, beyond the reach of those
       who would stand and wait for proof, help us to
       do the will of Christ, and come to know You in
       Him: Amen.

       *Also to be found at Fourth Sunday after Easter, second year
       (180), and at St Philip and St James (252)*

68   '*Believe me when I say that I am in the Father and
       the Father in me; or else accept the evidence of the
       deeds themselves.*'
       Lord Jesus, Your deeds matched Your words,
       and show us who You are; our deeds are smaller
       than our words and show us what we are; forgive
       our lack of love and of obedience, and grant us
       the help of Your Spirit of truth and strength to
       be with us for ever: Amen.

JOHN 15.1–5   **First Sunday after Trinity**

69   ' *. . . every fruiting branch he cleans . . .* '
       God of the living, prune from our lives all weak,
       diseased and useless growth, and keep our
       thoughts and actions rooted in our Lord, that
       love and joy may multiply in our lives and in the
       world, to Your glory: Amen.

       Also to be found at St Matthias (249)

70   '*I am the vine and you are the branches.*'
      Lord of the harvest, You have planted us in the
      world and we have turned it into a desert,
      producing hate and strife; graft us into our Lord
      and feed us on His word, that the desert may
      burst into flower and we may produce love, joy,
      peace, and all fruits of the Spirit: Amen.

JOHN 15.6–11   Second Sunday after Trinity

71   '*He who does not dwell in me is thrown away like a
      withered branch.*'
      Lord, if we leave Your presence we leave life
      itself; keep us in Your love and truth and feed us
      daily with the word of life, for the sake of Your
      glory in the world: Amen.

72   '*If you dwell in me, and my words dwell in you,
      ask what you will, and you shall have it.*'
      Lord and Father, fill us with such love for Your
      Son that our greatest need is to ask for His will
      to be done, and our greatest reward the joy and
      peace of His presence: Amen.

73   *'This is my commandment: love one another as I
       have loved you.'*
       Lord Jesus, You died in love and rose in power;
       transplant in us a new heart of love and send us
       out new people, strong to heal others by the
       power which healed us; life laid down in love:
       Amen.

74   *'This is my commandment: love one another as I
       have loved you.'*
       Father God, grant us the twin gifts of obedience
       and love, that we may in love lay our lives at
       Your feet, and in obedience take Your love to
       others, through the one who loved us and made
       us free, Jesus Christ our Saviour: Amen.

MATTHEW 19.16–26   **Fourth Sunday after Trinity**

75   *' . . . he went away with a heavy heart; for he was
       a man of great wealth.'*
       Lord, save us from the sorrow of keeping our
       possessions and losing You; keep before us a
       vision of Your love, the love which makes all
       things possible, even our free response to Your
       death on the Cross: Amen.

       *Also to be found at Fourteenth Sunday after Trinity, second
       year (218)*

76   '. . . a rich man will find it hard to enter the
      kingdom of heaven.'
      Lord of life, save us from the death of living for
      ourselves, and the loneliness of loving only
      ourselves, but give us grace to leave everything at
      Your invitation and enter the larger life of Your
      kingdom, the community of love and joy for
      ever: Amen.

      *Also to be found at First Sunday after Trinity, second year
      (191)*

LUKE 15.11–32   Fifth Sunday after Trinity

77   '*I will set off and go to my father and say to him,
      "Father, I have sinned . . . "* '
      Father God, You gave us the world, and we have
      wasted it and used its resources selfishly; show us
      the way back to a new beginning, come in love to
      meet us, and make us a new people fit for a new
      heaven and a new earth: Amen.

78   '*But he was angry and refused to go in.*'
      Father God, You love all men, and we love
      chiefly the lovable, forgive our lack of love;
      expand our hearts and help us to rejoice when the
      poor, the incompetent and the undeserving
      exceed us in love and go first into Your kingdom:
      Amen.

79   *'The master was so moved with pity that he let the
       man go and remitted the debt.'*
       Lord, save us from fear, fear of the inner depths
       of the mind; show us the matching depth of Your
       forgiveness, and fill us with the love which
       reaches every corner of the universe: Amen.

       *Also to be found at Twenty fourth Sunday after Trinity,
       second year (238)*

80   *' . . . forgive your brother from your hearts.'*
       Lord God, You loved the world at the cost of
       sending Your Son; send us Your measureless
       love, that we may forgive other people with no
       thought of the cost, for the sake of the one who
       died and rose again for our forgiveness: Amen.

JOHN 15.16–27   **Seventh Sunday after Trinity**

81   *'As they persecuted me, they will persecute
       you . . . '*
       Lord Jesus, Your love generates love; send us
       Your Spirit, and send us where wrong breeds
       wrong, to break the cycle of evil as You broke it
       once for all, by love crucified: Amen.

       *Also to be found at Seventh Sunday after Trinity, second
       year (203)*

82   *'But when your Advocate has come . . . he will bear witness to me.'*
Lord Jesus, living demonstration of the Father's love, support us by Your Spirit, that we, Your followers, may advertise Your strength and not our weakness, Your love and not our selfishness, to those who stretch us beyond our human limits: Amen.

Also to be found at Twelfth Sunday after Trinity, second year (214)

JOHN 17.11–19   Eighth Sunday after Trinity

83   *'I am to stay no longer in the world, but they are still in the world . . . '*
Send us, Holy Spirit of God, to speak where we may be heard and to live where we may be seen, that Christ may be known today in the place where things happen, in the heart of this modern age: Amen.

Also to be found at Second Sunday in Advent, second year (125)

84   *'I pray thee, not to take them out of the world, but to keep them from the evil one.'*
Lord, You prayed for us at all times and in Gethsemane; lock our separate lives together and help us to pray, each one for the other, that we may suffer as one, rejoice as one, fight evil as one, and as one body take Your message to the world: Amen.

85   '*He poured water into a basin and began to wash
     his disciples' feet . . .* '
     Lord, make us a community where each one
     loves the others, each one serves the others, and
     all are happy to take the lowest place, that in
     living as You lived we may turn our competitive
     world upside down, for the sake of Your love:
     Amen.

86   '*Peter said, "I will never let you wash my feet".*'
     Lord, Your love is larger than space and deeper
     than the human mind; save us from moulding it
     to fit our small response, but help our small
     response to grow, until we come to full
     obedience: Amen.

JOHN 13.33–36   **Tenth Sunday after Trinity**

87   '*As I have loved you, so you are to love one
     another.*'
     Lord, You loved us, and love took You to the
     Cross; help us to take the path of love and
     suffering, putting the good of others always above
     our own, for the sake of Your love, and in the
     power of Your resurrection: Amen.

88   *'Lord, where are you going?'*
Lord, Your love goes beyond death and beyond
suffering; help us to love one another beyond all
reasonable bounds, to explore the meaning of the
universe by dying for one another, and so to
come to our eternal home: Amen.

JOHN 17.20–26   Eleventh Sunday after Trinity

89   *' . . . may they all be one . . . '*
Lord, teach us to pray, and send Your Spirit to
graft us together a million living cells growing in
truth and love, that we may be in the world a
unity, the living and growing body of Christ, our
Lord and head: Amen.

90   *'The glory which thou gavest me I have given to
them . . . '*
Father God, Your glory left the temple and shone
from the Cross; send us out from our churches
into Your world, to be one body living for You,
suffering for You, and making Your glory
visible to men: Amen.

91   ' . . . *your Advocate . . . I will send him to*
       you . . . '
       Father God, You have made us alive in body;
       make us alive in spirit; that we may not stand
       like skeletons guarding our view of the truth, but
       may live joyfully and freely in this world, and be
       the home of your Spirit, the home of living truth
       for ever: Amen.

92   ' . . . *he will . . . show where wrong and right and*
       judgement lie . . . '
       Lord God, in an age where evil has many faces
       and goes by gentle names, send Your Spirit into
       our hearts to light the face of Christ, that we may
       live as seeing Him, and carry His name in the
       world: Amen.

LUKE 10.25–37   **Thirteenth Sunday after Trinity**

93   '*Love the Lord your God with all your heart . . .* '
       Lord and Father, whose love flows through us
       like a river, sweep away the barriers which
       obstruct the flow, that we may give Your love
       free passage through our lives to other people:
       Amen.

       Also to be found at Sixth Sunday after Trinity, second year
       (201)

94 '. . . *do that and you will live.*'
Lord, You sent Your Son to bring us life; send
us Your Spirit of love, which binds us to live as
Christ lived, and frees us to give our time and
our money, our present and our future, to our
neighbours, for Your sake: Amen.

Also to be found at Sixth Sunday after Trinity, second year
(202)

MARK 10.2–16   **Fourteenth Sunday after Trinity**

95 '*It was because your minds were closed that he
made this rule for you.*'
Lord of the universe, we make our own rules
because we cannot keep Your laws; make us new
people, fit for a new heaven and a new earth,
that we may live in harmony with all creation
and with our God: Amen.

96 '*Let the children come to me; do not try to stop
them . . .* '
Lord of life and love, who would not be
shrouded in convention and hidden from the
young, help us to see You as you are, and to
come, old and young, into Your kingdom
together, one in Your resurrection and one in
Your love: Amen.

97   *'Pay Caesar what is due to Caesar, and pay God
     what is due to God.'*
     Lord of all that changes and all that remains the
     same, keep our hearts fixed in You while our
     lives are spent changing society by loving our
     neighbours as ourselves, through the power of
     the Spirit: Amen.

98   *'Pay Caesar what is due to Caesar, and pay God
     what is due to God.'*
     Holy Spirit of God, when our love for our
     neighbour conflicts with our duty to the State,
     make us like our Lord, who loved men and was
     killed by the State, who loved God and was
     raised from the dead: Amen.

MATTHEW 7.21–29   **Sixteenth Sunday after Trinity**

99   *'Not everyone who calls me "Lord, Lord" will
     enter the kingdom of heaven, but only those who
     do the will of my heavenly Father.'*
     God of all being, maintaining all that exists,
     show us Your will and help us to obey, that in
     our present doing we may find our eternal being,
     and be Your children now and for ever: Amen.

100 *'The rain came down, the floods rose, the wind
blew, and beat upon that house.'*
Lord of all power and goodness, when evil forces
try to break our minds, take our deepest motives
and align them with Your will, that the bedrock of
our being may be full obedience: Amen.

MATTHEW 5.21–26   Seventeenth Sunday after Trinity

101 ' . . . *leave your gift where it is before the altar.'*
Lord, You fill all things, give us grace to look for
You where You are closest at hand, not in
consecrated buildings, but in the hearts of those
with whom we do not get on: Amen.

102 ' . . . *go and make your peace with your
brother . . .* '
Lord, give us the courage to make amends for the
hurt we cause to others, and make us fit for Your
kingdom, where love alone inspires all thought,
and action, through Christ in whom we are
forgiven: Amen.

103 *'They made a big haul of fish . . . As soon as they
     had brought the boats to land, they left
     everything . . . '*
     Lord, You call us to love people more than
     things; help us to abandon even the gifts You
     have given us when You call us to follow You
     and bring others into your kingdom: Amen.

104 *' . . . they left everything and followed him.'*
     Lord, Your abundant love is a free gift to the
     undeserving; help us to respond like Peter, and
     leave the known for the unknown, security for
     danger, success for the risk of failure, for the joy
     of living in Your presence and doing Your will:
     Amen.

JOHN 17.1–10   **Nineteenth Sunday after Trinity**

105 *'I have glorified thee on earth by completing the
     work which thou gavest me to do . . . '*
     Lord of glory, who finished the Father's work,
     give us grace to finish the work we have begun,
     the spreading of Your Good News to all the
     world in our generation: Amen.

106 *'I pray for them . . .'*
Lord, You prayed in Galilee, Gethsemane, and on
the Cross; help us into the presence of the Father
and teach us to pray, that we may know and love
and obey our living God, and see His kingdom
come on earth: Amen.

*Also to be found at Fifteenth Sunday after Trinity, second
year (219)*

LUKE 9.51–62   Twentieth Sunday after Trinity

107 *' . . . you must go and announce the kingdom of
God.'*
Lord of love, give us the enterprise to go as You
command, to the busy, the scornful, the unlikely
and the uninviting, with the good news of the
kingdom of joy which is open to all: Amen.

108 *' . . . you must go and announce the kingdom of
God.'*
Lord, pour out Your peace through us to others,
that we may be living invitations, active
messengers, commending Your kingdom of joy
which is open to all: Amen.

109 *'Our fathers worshipped on this mountain, but you
     Jews say . . . '*
     Lord, when modern thought and ancient
     tradition meet to confuse our minds, be our guide;
     focus the light of Your truth not on outer
     conflict but on the darker corners of our inner
     lives, that we may be fully open to Your presence
     and worship You in spirit and in truth: Amen.

     *Also to be found at Sixth Sunday after Epiphany, second
     year (147)*

110 *'The woman answered, "I know that Messiah . . .
     is coming . . . ". Jesus said, "I am he, I who am
     speaking to you now".'*
     Lord of all time, You answer our hopes for the
     future in the present; show us now our king and
     deliverer, save us now from our sins, and make
     us now heirs of the future kingdom, growing like
     our Lord: Amen.

**MATTHEW 20.1–15   Twenty Second Sunday after
                      Trinity**

111 *'Go and join the others in the vineyard . . . '*
     Lord of the harvest, send us, Your workers, into
     every area of modern life, and give us grace to
     commend Your love to all men by our love for
     one another, that we may bring in Your harvest
     and rejoice in Your kingdom: Amen.

     *Also to be found at Fifth Sunday after Epiphany, second
     year (145)*

112 *'I will pay you a fair wage . . . '*
Lord Jesus Christ, in whose kingdom equal pay
for equal work is unknown, but the great gift of
salvation is given to all, give us such joy in
serving You that differentials are forgotten and
God dwells in us as we love one another: Amen.

*Also to be found at Fifth Sunday after Epiphany, second
year (146)*

JOHN 1.1–14   Twenty Third Sunday after Trinity

113 *'But to all who did receive him . . . he gave the
right to become children of God . . . '*
Lord Jesus Christ, You came from the Father
into the world and finished the work He gave you
to do; be born in us that we may die with You
and share in Your resurrection: Amen.

Also to be found at Christmas Day, second year (131)

114 *'So the Word became flesh; he came to dwell
among us and we saw his glory . . . '*
Lord Jesus, light of men, born at Christmas time
to be received by some and rejected by others,
bring into our lives the light of forgiveness and of
new life, that as children of God we may grow
daily in grace and truth: Amen.

Also to be found at Christmas Day, second year (132)

115   '*This Son of Man must be lifted up . . .*'
Father God, You lifted Your Son on the Cross
above all history and raised Him from the dead;
draw us into His timeless presence, draw us to
love Him, to leave the sin He has conquered, and
to live for Him now and for ever: Amen.
Also to be found at Fifth Sunday in Lent, first year (44)

116   '*It was not to judge the world that God sent his
Son into the world . . .*'
Father God, when our sins are stronger than our
faith and we hide from Your light, have mercy;
give us again such trust in Your love and
goodness that we return to our Lord, the light of
the world who exposes in order to heal and not
to condemn: Amen.

JOHN 8.51–58   Twenty Fifth Sunday after Trinity

117   '*Jesus said, "Before Abraham was born, I am.*'
Lord of time, Lord from before our birth to
beyond our death, help us to know You in each
moment, so that keeping Your word, we may
live now in the free and greater life of God:
Amen.

118 *'Jesus said, " . . . before Abraham was born, I
am". They picked up stones to throw at him . . . '*
Lord, You came to show God to men and were
not afraid of their anger; take from us the wish
to speak in inoffensive whispers in an
unwelcoming world, and make us strong to speak
of You boldly, in Your name: Amen.

JOHN 6.27–35   Twenty Sixth Sunday after Trinity

119 *'You must work, not for this perishable food, but
for the food that lasts, the food of eternal life.'*
Lord, You healed the sick and fed the healthy,
You know and meet all our needs; keep us from
following You for the joy and strength you offer,
and help us in love to take the way of the
Cross: Amen.

Also to be found at Quinquagesima, first year (32)

120 *'I am the bread of life . . . '*
Lord, who drew crowds into the desert to hear the
words of eternal life, draw us into your presence
daily, to feed not on present worries and future
longings, but on Your eternal truth and strength:
Amen.

121   '*Keep awake, then, for you do not know on what
day your Lord is to come.*'
Lord, may the vision of Your future coming
shape our present lives, that we may pray today
and work today in joyful expectation of
tomorrow, ready at all times for our King and
Judge: Amen.

*Also to be found at Nineteenth Sunday after Trinity, second
year (228)*

122   '*Hold yourselves ready . . .* '
Lord Jesus, who when the solar system ends will
shine brighter than the sun, help us now to make
the light of Your presence known in all the
world, for the sake of Your love: Amen.

*Also to be found at Twenty Sixth Sunday after Trinity,
second year (241)*

Sundays
and Major Festivals
second year

123   ' . . . *when I was hungry, you gave me food . . .* '
Lord God, Your Son lives and suffers in today's
people; send us in love to those who need our
time and our care, our comfort and our
possessions, that we all may grow to be fully
human, fully like our Lord: Amen.

124   ' . . . *anything you did for one of my brothers here*
. . . you did for me.'
Lord of fire and judgement, set our hearts alight
with love, not fear, that we may gladly spend our
lives for others, seeing in them not the Son of
Man our Judge, but the Son of Man our
brother: Amen.

LUKE 4.14–21   Second Sunday in Advent

125   ' . . . *all eyes in the synagogue were fixed on him.*
He began to speak . . . '
Send us, Holy Spirit of God, to speak where we
may be heard and to live where we may be seen,
that Christ may be known today in the place
where things happen, in the heart of this modern
age: Amen.

Also to be found at Eighth Sunday after Trinity, first year
(83)

126 ‘ *"Today,"* he said, *"in your very hearing this text has come true".'*
Lord, You are fully at home and fully human in every age and culture; come to us in our own day, God in our own home town, God in our lives, and grant us the power to recognize you at your coming: Amen.

MATTHEW 11.2–15   **Third Sunday in Advent**

127 *‘Are you the one who is to come?'*
Lord Jesus, who came once, the great fact of the past, and will come again, the great fact of the future, be with us now in the time between. Bind together our present, past and future, that saved by You, made whole by You, and judged by You, we may share with You in Your glory: Amen.

128 *‘Go and tell John what you hear and see . . .'*
Lord Jesus, who came in love to heal the blind, the deaf and the dying, open our eyes to the Way, and our ears to the Truth, that our lives may be spent spreading the good news we have seen and heard, until You come again in power to judge the world: Amen.

129   '*Do not be afraid to take Mary home with you as
your wife.*'
Living Lord, grant us the ability to change our
minds, and the courage always to live under the
direction of Your Spirit: Amen.

130   '*The virgin will conceive and bear a son, and he
shall be called Emmanuel, a name which means
God is with us.*'
Holy Spirit, Lord of life, bringer of Christ, come
into our world; show us Christ in time past, born
of Mary, and show us Christ in time present,
born in us, to make us His body doing His work
in the world: Amen.

JOHN 1.1–14   Christmas Day

131   '*But to all who did receive him . . . he gave the
right to become children of God . . .* '
Lord Jesus Christ, You came from the Father into
the world and finished the work He gave you to
do; be born in us that we may die with You and
share in Your resurrection: Amen.

*Also to be found at Twenty third Sunday after Trinity, first
year (113)*

132 '*So the Word became flesh; he came to dwell*
      among us and we saw his glory . . .'
      Lord Jesus, light of men, born at Christmas time
      to be received by some and rejected by others,
      bring into our lives the light of forgiveness and of
      new life, that as children of God we may grow
      daily in grace and truth: Amen.

      Also to be found at Twenty third Sunday after Trinity, first
      year (114)

MATTHEW 2.1–12   First Sunday after Christmas

133 '*We observed the rising of his star, and we have*
      come to pay him homage . . .'
      Lord Jesus, worshipped by foreigners who read
      the signs of the times and recognized a king,
      teach us to read the signs of our own times which
      mark Your presence in this world, and lead us to
      live our lives in obedience to Your kingly rule:
      Amen.

      Also to be found at First Sunday after Christmas, first year
      (11)

134 ' *. . . then they opened their treasures and offered*
      him gifts . . .'
      Lord Jesus, You received gifts from strangers;
      help us who are adopted into God's family to
      obey You as king, to worship You as Lord, to
      share in Your death and to rejoice with You in
      Your resurrection: Amen.

      Also to be found at First Sunday after Christmas, first year
      (12)

135 ' . . . *and after three days they found him sitting in the temple . . .* '
Lord God, whose Son came of age and looked for knowledge in His Father's house; help us to search for truth where truth is to be found, to grow in grace as we do Your will, and to come to full maturity in Christ, full of grace and truth: Amen.

136 '*Your father and I have been searching for you in great anxiety.*'
Lord and Father, help us to hear Your call to others as clearly as we hear our own, and to trust You with the lives of others as we trust You with our own: Amen.

JOHN 1.29–34   First Sunday after Epiphany

137 '*I saw the Spirit coming down from heaven like a dove . . .* '
Holy Spirit, Lord of our lives, bring us to know You in our whole being, in what we are and in what we do; bring us the power to be the children of God, and to do the work of God, in the name of the Son, our Lord and brother: Amen.
Also to be found at Septuagesima, first year (28)

138   *' . . . this is he who is to baptize in Holy Spirit.'*
     Lord of the Church, who baptized us into one
     body, to share one life and one purpose in the
     world, deepen our trust in Your Spirit, that He
     may lead us deeper into truth, and bring us in
     love closer to You and to one another: Amen.

JOHN 1.35–51   **Second Sunday after Epiphany**

139   *'The first thing he did was to find his brother*
     Simon. He said to him, "We have found the
     Messiah".'
     Lord Jesus, the Good News who comes in
     person, our encounter with You yesterday has
     gone like yesterday's news; meet us today, Lord,
     and fill us with today's news for today's people,
     Your loving invitation to all who look for truth;
     'Come and see': Amen.

140   *'Philip went to find Nathanael . . . '*
     Lord Jesus, You have met us in our whole being;
     help us to share ourselves with other people, so
     that in showing our secret weaknesses we also
     share our single strength – that in meeting You
     we have met God: Amen.

141 *'There he found in the temple the dealers in cattle,
     sheep and pigeons, and the money-changers seated
     at their tables.'*
     Lord, You drove from the temple those whose aim
     it was to make money; drive from our hearts the
     desire to own things and to do well in this life.
     May we, who are Your church and temple, be
     filled with You alone, and show Your glory to
     the world: Amen.

142 *'Jesus . . . drove them out of the temple . . . '*
     All-powerful indwelling God, farther than the
     farthest star and nearer than our most secret
     thought, sweep from our minds our substitutes
     for living prayer, that Christ may fill our lives
     and bring us to His glory, which He shared with
     You before the world was made: Amen.

JOHN 4.7–14   Fourth Sunday after Epiphany

143 *'Jesus said to her, "Give me a drink".'*
     Lord of living water, who depended on a
     stranger for a drink, help us to receive as freely
     as we give, that the stranger who supplies our
     need may be our friend, and together we may
     drink the water of life: Amen.

144 '*The water that I shall give him will be an inner
     spring always welling up for eternal life.*'
     Lord Jesus, our inner spring of living water, we
     would drink from You today, believe in You
     today, and work for You today; grant us today a
     surge of new life, welling up and spilling into a
     dry world, for the sake of Your love: Amen.

MATTHEW 20.1–15   Fifth Sunday after Epiphany

145 '*Go and join the others in the vineyard . . .*'
     Lord of the harvest, send us, Your workers, into
     every area of modern life, and give us grace to
     commend Your love to all men by our love for
     one another, that we may bring in Your harvest
     and rejoice in Your kingdom: Amen.

     *Also to be found at Twenty second Sunday after Trinity,
     first year (111)*

146 '*I will pay you a fair wage . . .*'
     Lord Jesus Christ, in whose kingdom equal pay
     for equal work is unknown, but the great gift of
     salvation is given to all, give us also such joy in
     serving You that differentials are forgotten, and
     God dwells in us as we love one another: Amen.

     *Also to be found at Twenty second Sunday after Trinity,
     first year (112)*

147 *'Our fathers worshipped on this mountain, but you
Jews say . . . '*
Lord, when modern thought and ancient
tradition meet to confuse our minds, be our guide,
focus the light of Your truth not on outer
conflict, but on the darker corners of our inner
lives, that we may be fully open to Your
presence and worship You in spirit and in truth:
Amen.

*Also to be found at Twenty first Sunday after Trinity, first
year (109)*

148 *'The woman answered, "I know that Messiah . . .
is coming . . . ". Jesus said, "I am he, I who am
speaking to you now".'*
Lord of all time, You answer our hopes for the
future in the present; show us now our King and
deliverer, save us now from our sins, and make
us now heirs of the future kingdom, growing like
our Lord: Amen.

*Also to be found at Twenty first Sunday after Trinity, first
year (110)*

LUKE 8.4–15   Septuagesima

149 *'A sower went out to sow his seed.'*
Lord, You have given us seed to sow; teach us
not to despair over the state of the ground or
limit our activities to fertile spots, but to go into
every part of our society and spread Your word
of life to all: Amen.

150 '*Some of the seed fell into good soil, and grew, and
yielded a hundredfold.*'
Lord of life, You leave us free to kill or stunt or
choke the living word You sow; help us daily to
clear the way for growth, that we may be filled
with Your abundant life now and for ever: Amen.

MARK 1.35–45   Sexagesima

151 '*He went away to a lonely spot and remained there
in prayer.*'
Lord, when our minds are troubled and we need
Your presence more than sleep, help us to pray;
meet us in the dark and silent places of the mind;
fill us with light and joy; and bring to our waking
lives the power to do Your work: Amen.

152 '*Jesus stretched out his hand, touched him, and said
" . . . be clean again".*'
Lord Jesus, You loved the ugly and the deformed,
and turned lepers into living evidence for God;
touch our inner deformities and send us out
healed, living demonstrations of Your truth and
love: Amen.

153 ' . . . *he said to them, "Let us cross over to the
other side of the lake." . . . A heavy squall came
on . . .* '
Lord Jesus, You led Your followers into a fierce
storm; help us to follow You into the hurricane
zones of this life, where alone Your power
becomes apparent, for the sake of Your glorious
kingdom of peace: Amen.

154 '*Have you no faith even now?*'
Lord, Your power is spread through all the
universe; expand our faith, until we know You
not in isolated acts, but in the very fabric of our
lives, and in the lives of others: Amen.

LUKE 18.9–14   **Ash Wednesday**

155 '*Those who were sure of their own goodness . . .* '
Lord God, ground of our being, forgive us for
blinding ourselves to our own worst faults; open
our eyes to see the depth of self-love, and open
our hearts to know the depth of Your mercy, for
the sake of Jesus Christ, our Saviour: Amen.

156 *'But the other kept his distance, and would not
even raise his eyes to heaven . . . '*
Lord and Father, when our sins and failures
overwhelm us, and we feel far from your presence,
show us the face of Christ, in whom we are
forgiven: Amen.

LUKE 4.1–13   First Sunday in Lent

157 *'Jesus . . . was led by the Spirit up and down the
wilderness, and tempted by the devil.'*
Lord, You were tested by a choice of three ways
to do your work; help us in our own lives always
to choose the fourth way, the way of self-giving
and of the Cross: Amen.

Also to be found at First Sunday in Lent, first year (35)

158 *'The devil . . . showed him in a flash all the
kingdoms of the world.'*
Lord, You have sent us into the world to make
followers from every nation; keep us from
offering the hungry nothing but bread, from
presenting proofs instead of a Person, and from
serving the forces of this world in the hope that
they will serve us, Your messengers: Amen.

Also to be found at First Sunday in Lent, first year (36)

159 ' . . . *Jesus cured him, restoring both speech and
     sight . . .* '
     Lord, who never left a man half-healed, send us
     Your Spirit, that we, whom You have made
     whole, may wholly finish every task You call us
     to begin: Amen.

160 ' . . . *the Pharisees . . . said, "It is only by
     Beelzebub prince of devils that this man drives the
     devils out".* '
     Holy Spirit of God, when evil seems good and
     good seems evil, come and show us the difference;
     Holy giver of life, when we know what is good
     but cannot follow it, come and give us strength,
     for the sake of Christ, our deliverer: Amen.

LUKE 9.18–27   **Third Sunday in Lent**

161 ' *"And you,"* he said, *"who do you say I am?".
     Peter answered, "God's Messiah".* '
     Lord of truth, teach us to live each moment
     recognizing you as king, so that everywhere we go
     our words and our working lives make plain the
     King who died in love and rose in power, to
     bring us to God: Amen.

     Also to be found at Third Sunday in Lent, first year (39)

162 '*If anyone wishes to be a follower of mine, he must leave self behind; day after day he must take up his cross . . . *'
Lord Jesus Christ, who died for us, open the inward ear of our minds to hear Your voice speaking of the Cross, that we who come after You may die daily in Your service: Amen.

LUKE 9.28–36   Fourth Sunday in Lent

163 '*. . . the appearance of his face changed and his clothes became dazzling white.*'
Living Lord, who links us with eternity, grant us the vision which passes in a flash but lasts for ever, and grant us all our lives to follow you: Amen.

Also to be found at Fourth Sunday in Lent, first year (41) and at The Transfiguration of our Lord (259)

164 '*. . . they saw his glory . . . *'
Loving Father, in our suffering send us strength; show us the glory at the heart of pain, the glory of Christ, the sufferer who died in love, that we who are freed by His death may freely love Him through death to resurrection: Amen.

Also to be found at Fourth Sunday in Lent, first year (42)

165   *'Grant us the right to sit in state with you, one at
      your right and the other at your left.'*
      Lord, You are our life; save us from making You
      our career, that we may always be willing to take
      the lowest place, seeing You in everyone we
      serve, for the sake of Your love: Amen.

166   *' . . . to sit at my right or left is not for me to
      grant . . . '*
      Lord Jesus, make us, like James, able to follow
      You to death not for a place in heaven, but
      because we have seen You on earth. Amen.

      Also to be found at St James the Apostle (258)

MATTHEW 21.1–11   **Palm Sunday**

167   *'They were now nearing Jerusalem . . . '*
      Lord, You rode straight into the power of the
      enemy to suffer and die; give us the strength to
      follow You to the centres of opposition in this
      world, and the confidence which confronts power
      with love: Amen.

      *Also to be found at Palm Sunday, first year (45) and at
      Twenty fifth Sunday after Trinity, second year (239)*

168 *'Then the crowd . . . raised the shout: "Hosanna to
the Son of David!"'*
Lord Jesus, Word of God and Lord of history,
You were welcomed as prophet and king by those
who understood in part; give us grace to welcome
You into Your kingdom within us, that we may
grow in knowledge of truth and be ruled by Your
love for ever: Amen.

JOHN 19.1–37   Good Friday

169 *'Then time after time they came up to him, crying,
"Hail, King of the Jews!", and struck him on the
face.'*
Lord of every power in the universe, who did not
resist death on the Cross, give us such trust in
Your victory that we may meet all who choose
evil with non-violent love: Amen.

Also to be found at Good Friday, first year (47)

170 *'He said, "It is accomplished!" He bowed his head
and gave up his spirit.'*
All-loving God, whose Son died to free us from
the grip of evil, keep us alive and free in His
kingdom, dead to self and abundantly alive to our
Lord and King who rules for ever: Amen.

Also to be found at Good Friday, first year (48)

171 ' . . . *Mary of Magdala and the other Mary came*
     to look at the grave.'
     Lord and Father, send Your Spirit into Your
     world-wide Church, that those who approach it
     in sadness and despair may find the gloriously
     living body of Christ, and all men may believe:
     Amen.

     Also to be found at Easter Day, first year (49)

172 '*He is not here; he has been raised again . . .* '
     Lord God, You freed Christ from death once for
     all time; free us each day from our old self, that
     we may live the new life of Christ now and for
     ever: Amen.

     Also to be found at Easter Day, first year (50)

JOHN 6.35–40   **First Sunday after Easter**

173 '*I am the bread of life . . .* '
     Lord, You have called us into the great fellowship
     of those hungry for Your word; old and young,
     black and white, rich and poor; teach us to share
     all things in common and to serve one another
     with the bread of life: Amen.

174   '*Whoever comes to me shall never be hungry . . .*'
Lord, You drew crowds into the desert to hear
the words of eternal life; draw us into Your
presence daily to feed not on present worries and
future longings, but on Your eternal truth and
strength, whose meat and drink was finishing the
Father's work: Amen.

JOHN 10.7–18   Second Sunday after Easter

175 '*The hireling . . . abandons the sheep and runs
away . . .*'
Lord and Saviour, keep us from following leaders
whose lives lack love and whose ideals lack power,
but help us to be faithful to You, who died in
love and rose in power to bring us to God: Amen.

176   '*I lay down my life for the sheep . . .*'
Lord, You lead your followers through death to
resurrection; help us daily to listen to Your voice,
and to lay down our lives for You as You laid
down Your life for us: Amen.

177 '*If you had been here, sir, my brother would not
    have died.*'
    Lord, when tragedy breaks up our lives, come to
    us as You came to Martha, who reproached You
    for the past and found that You could change the
    future, through the power of the resurrection:
    Amen.

178 '*I am the resurrection and I am life,*'
    Lord, Your love brought Lazarus from the tomb;
    bring Your Church into the light of day to live
    and work for You, that faith may come to life
    in those who see our resurrection: Amen.

JOHN 14.1-11   **Fourth Sunday after Easter**

179 '*Lord, we do not know where you are going, so how
    can we know the way?*'
    Lord, You returned to the Father by way of the
    Cross; when we fear for the future show us the
    path of love, and lead us a step at a time until
    You receive us in Your Father's house: Amen.

180 *'I am the way . . . '*
God of all knowledge, beyond the reach of those
who would stand and wait for proof, help us to
do the will of Christ, and come to know You in
Him: Amen.

*Also to be found at St Philip and St James, Apostles (252)
and at Trinity Sunday, first year (67)*

JOHN 16.12–24   Fifth Sunday after Easter

181 *'We do not know what he means.'*
Lord, You see time whole where we see only part
of the present and part of the past; help us to
understand Your words, and bring us through
puzzlement, doubt, and sadness into the joy of
Your presence for ever: Amen.

182 *'But though you will be plunged in grief, your grief
will be turned to joy.'*
Father God, Your Son was tortured and killed
on our account; give us the strength to share that
suffering which turns to joy, and that death which
is swallowed up in resurrection: Amen.

*Also to be found at Twenty sixth Sunday after Trinity,
second year (242)*

183 *'Go forth therefore . . . '*
Lord God, send Your love into our hearts, that
we may gladly go into the world which Christ has
left and spread the good news of His kingdom in
the power which He has given us: Amen.

Also to be found at Ascension Day, first year (61)

184 *' . . . make all nations my disciples . . . '*
Father God, as there is one Christ in heaven,
make us one body on earth, that we may do the
will of our Lord and Head in the joy of unity,
and make Him known throughout the world, one
Saviour and one God: Amen.

Also to be found at Ascension Day, first year (62)

LUKE 24.44–53   **Sunday after Ascension Day**

185 *' . . . until you are armed with the power from
above.'*
Lord God, You brought the universe into a
unity in Christ, and this is the measure of Your
power; unite Your people on earth with Your
Son in heaven, that in Your power we may bring
Him to all people: Amen.

*Also to be found at Sunday after Ascension Day, first year
(64)*

186 ' . . . *until you are armed with the power from above.*'
Lord God, You send us out to spread good news, and we are hindered by our inner enemies, fear, selfishness, uncertainty; Lord Christ, forgive, arm us with Your power, conquer these contradictions of Your love, and make us fit to bring Your news to others: Amen.

Also to be found at Sunday after Ascension Day, first year (63)

JOHN 14.15–27   Whit Sunday

187 ' . . . *the Holy Spirit . . . will teach you everything, and will call to mind all that I have told you.*'
Lord of a technical age, where knowledge is stored in computers and human minds are left blank, restore our will to learn and send us Your Spirit, that all the words of Your Son may be printed on our hearts and in our lives: Amen.

Also to be found at Whit Sunday, first year (65)

188 '*Peace is my parting gift to you . . .* '
God of an explosive world, where bombs and weapons talk, send into our hearts the dynamite of Your Spirit, that we may know power and peace together, and speak of You to all people in ways which reach the centre of their being: Amen.

Also to be found at Whit Sunday, first year (66)

189 *'I thank thee, Father, Lord of heaven and earth, for
    hiding these things from the learned and wise . . . '*
    Lord, keep our lives simple in a complex world,
    and help us to live by the single rule of love, that
    all the universe may be reunited with its Maker:
    Amen.

    *Also to be found at Sixth Sunday after Epiphany, first year
    (25) and at Twenty first Sunday after Trinity, second year
    (231)*

190 *'For my yoke is good to bear, my load is light.'*
    Lord God, free us from the yoke of institutional
    religion, and bring us each one to Him whose
    yoke is good to bear, that in fellowship with one
    another we may bring Christ to all people: Amen.

LUKE 14.15–24   First Sunday after Trinity

191 *'They began one and all to excuse themselves.'*
    Lord of life, save us from the death of living for
    ourselves, and the loneliness of loving only
    ourselves, but give us grace to leave everything at
    Your invitation and enter the larger life of Your
    kingdom, the community of joy and love for
    ever: Amen.

    *Also to be found at Fourth Sunday after Trinity, first year
    (76)*

192 ' . . . *bring me in the poor, the crippled, the blind
and the lame.*'
Lord, Your love is as large as the universe, with
room for all men; expand our hearts to welcome
into our lives the poor, the unlovely, the
inadequate and the stranger, who are first in
Your kingdom: Amen.

LUKE 8.41–55   Second Sunday after Trinity

193 '*She came up from behind and touched the edge of
his cloak . . .* '
Lord, do not leave us alone in an overcrowded
world, but keep us as close to You as to our
neighbours, that Your power may pass through
us to those whose lives touch ours: Amen.

194 '*Your daughter is dead . . .* '
Lord, forgive us for our despair, when evil seems
stronger than good and death is permanent and
life has lost its meaning; do not turn us out of
Your presence, but show us, as never before, the
power of Your resurrection: Amen.

195 *'Rejoice with me! . . . I have found my lost sheep.'*
Lord Jesus, You came to look for the lost and
live with the rejected: breathe into us Your love
and compassion, that we may live as You lived,
and rate Your joy in heaven above our image on
earth: Amen.

*Also to be found at Eighteenth Sunday after Trinity, second
year (226)*

196 *' . . . there will be greater joy in heaven over one
sinner who repents . . . '*
Lord Jesus, You love people as we love
possessions; bring us the gift of repentance, that
there may be joy in heaven as we follow You on
earth: Amen.

LUKE 17.11–19   Fourth Sunday after Trinity

197 *'The other nine, where are they?'*
Lord, You surround us with loving power, and
create the laws of the universe; expand our
understanding of the world and of Your love,
that in everything we may give thanks: Amen.

198 *'The other nine, where are they?'*
Lord, You healed those who showed no thanks;
teach us to be kind to the ungrateful, to love the
unlovely, and to be compassionate as our Father
is compassionate, who has made us sons of the
most High: Amen.

MARK 10.46–52   Fifth Sunday after Trinity

199 *'Many of the people told him to hold his
tongue . . . '*
Lord of all healing, give us Your own compassion
for other people, that we may never live lives
which bar from Your presence those who would
reach You, but rather may open the way for
Your healing power, for the sake of Your love:
Amen.

200 *'Jesus stopped and said, "Call him".'*
Lord, when we are strangers alone in the crowd,
call us into Your presence and make us whole;
restore our minds and bodies and restore our
love for people, that we may be fully alive to
others and fully alive to You: Amen.

201 ' *. . . love the Lord your God . . .* '
Lord and Father, whose love flows through us
like a river, sweep away the barriers which
obstruct the flow, that we may give Your love
free passage through our lives to other people:
Amen.

*Also to be found at Thirteenth Sunday after Trinity, first
year (93)*

202 '*Love your neighbour as yourself.*'
Lord, You sent Your Son to bring us life; send
us Your Spirit of love, which binds us to live as
Christ lived, and frees us to give our time and
our money, our present and our future, to our
neighbour, for Your sake: Amen.

*Also to be found at Thirteenth Sunday after Trinity, first
year (94)*

LUKE 6.27–38   **Seventh Sunday after Trinity**

203 '*Love your enemies . . .* '
Lord Jesus, Your love generates love; send us
Your Spirit, and send us where wrong breeds
wrong, to break the cycle of evil as You broke it
once and for all, by love crucified: Amen.

*Also to be found at Seventh Sunday after Trinity, first year
(81)*

204   '. . . *do good to those who hate you.*'
Lord Jesus, killed by hate and raised by love,
help us to be Your witnesses in a hostile world;
to show most love where there is most hate, and
to live united to one another until You come
again: Amen.

Also to be found at St Simon and St Jude, Apostles (266)

MARK 9.14–29   Eighth Sunday after Trinity

205 '*I asked your disciples to cast it out, but they
failed.*'
Lord, other people's problems fill us with
weakness and lack of faith; strengthen our prayers
and fill us with Your presence, that we may have
confidence in Your love and touch the needs of
others with Your power to heal: Amen.

206 '. . . *help me where faith falls short.*'
Lord, You care for all our needs; send us faith,
that we, who think our problems are great, may
trust in that which is greater, Your everlasting
power and mercy: Amen.

207   '*She took her place behind him, by his feet,*
      weeping.'
      Lord, save us from despair, the despair of
      knowing the inner depths of our minds; the
      depth of our sin; show us the matching depths of
      Your forgiveness, and fill us with the love which
      reaches every corner of the universe: Amen.

208   '*His feet were wetted with her tears and she wiped*
      them with her hair, kissing them and anointing
      them with myrrh.'
      Lord, who saved us, and loved us beyond death
      and beyond suffering; help us to love You beyond
      all reasonable bounds and to lay our lives at
      Your feet now and for ever: Amen.

209   '*If you had faith no bigger even than a mustard*
      seed, you could say to this mulberry tree . . .'
      Father God, may the words of Christ direct all
      we do, and the mind of Christ direct all we think,
      that we may obey You in all things and exercise
      Your power on earth, to the glory of Your name:
      Amen.

210 *'If you had faith no bigger even than a mustard
seed, you could say to this mulberry tree . . .'*
Lord, You came by faith to Gethsemane and the
Cross; fill us with faith like Yours, to bring us
beyond the doing of great things for God to total
obedience to the way of death, and total trust in
the power of resurrection: Amen.

MATTHEW 5.13–16   Eleventh Sunday after Trinity

211 *'You are salt to the world . . .'*
God of peace, send us where there is conflict;
God of joy, send us where there is despair; God
of love, send us where there is hate; and save us
from blending with the background You have
sent us to redeem, through Christ, our strength
and our Saviour: Amen.

212 *'You are light for all the world . . .'*
Lord of joy, we bring You our sadness; Lord of
peace, we bring You our troubled minds; Lord of
light, we bring You lives shadowed by
selfishness; light us with Your presence and send
us out to light the world: Amen.

213 ' . . . *they will flog you in the synagogues* . . . '
Lord God, You sent the Prince of Peace into a
violent world to be killed; send us into our world
of wealth, hunger and self-regard, that men may
explore the limits of Christ's love as we live and
die for others, in the power of Your Spirit:
Amen.

Also to be found at St Stephen (270)

214 ' . . . *you will be brought before governors and
kings . . . to testify before them* . . . '
Lord Jesus, living demonstration of the Father's
love, support us by Your Spirit, that we, Your
followers, may advertise Your strength and not
our weakness, Your love and not our selfishness,
to those who stretch us beyond our human
limits: Amen.

*Also to be found at Seventh Sunday after Trinity, first year
(82)*

LUKE 16.19–31   **Thirteenth Sunday after Trinity**

215 '*At his gate, covered with sores, lay a poor man
named Lazarus* . . . '
Lord and Father, transplant in us a new heart of
love, that we may see the hungry of the world
lying at our door, and may offer not what we can
spare but what they need, and be with them one
family: Amen.

216 ' . . . *they will pay no heed . . .* '
Lord Jesus, patient for ever, forgive Your people;
speak to those who choose to be deaf; give light
to those who choose to be blind, and send Your
Spirit to those who choose to do nothing, while
hearing Your word and seeing the needs of the
world: Amen.

LUKE 14.25–33   Fourteenth Sunday after Trinity

217 '*No one who does not carry his cross and come
with me can be a disciple of mine.*'
Lord Jesus Christ, who died for us, open the
inward ear of our minds to hear Your voice
speaking of the Cross, that we who come after
You may travel with You and die daily in Your
service: Amen.

Also to be found at Third Sunday in Lent, first year (40)

218 ' . . . *none of you can be a disciple of mine
without parting with all his possessions.*'
Lord, save us from the sorrow of keeping our
possessions and losing You; keep before us a
vision of Your love, the love which makes all
things possible, even our free response to Your
death on the Cross: Amen.

*Also to be found at Fourth Sunday after Trinity, first year
(75)*

219 *'Lord, teach us to pray . . .'*
Lord, You prayed in Galilee, Gethsemane, and
on the Cross; help us into the presence of the
Father and teach us to pray, that we may know
and obey our living God, and see His kingdom
come on earth: Amen.

*Also to be found at Nineteenth Sunday after Trinity, first
year (106)*

220 *' . . . seek, and you will find . . .'*
Lord of the universe, help us to look for You in
the very depths of our own being, and to find
You in the silence which lies deeper than
thought: Amen.

LUKE 7.1–10   Sixteenth Sunday after Trinity

221 *'But say the word and my servant will be cured. I
know, for in my position I am myself under
orders . . .'*
Lord Jesus, obedient to the Father in every detail
of a crowded life, send us Your orders and help
us to obey, that we may know Your truth, be the
home of Your Spirit, and finish the work You
have given us to do: Amen.

222 '*I tell you, nowhere, even in Israel, have I found faith like this.*'
Lord, You found faith in unexpected people, religious fellow-travellers of the times; help us to live in Your Church so close to those outside it that we may know and share true faith across the border: Amen.

MATTHEW 25.14–29   Seventeenth Sunday after Trinity

223 '*It is like a man going abroad, who called his servants and put his capital in their hands . . .*'
Father God, You have given us gifts; help us to use them adventurously; to expose ourselves to despair and lack of faith; to risk losing our trust in You that trust in You might multiply in the world, and Your kingdom come: Amen.

224 ' *. . . to one he gave five bags of gold, to another two, to another one . . .* '
Lord Jesus, we are born unequal in many things, make us equal in this one thing; our determination to spend our lives for You, and to use every faculty we have to spread the good news of Your kingdom, until You come again: Amen.

225   *'He was eager to see what Jesus looked like, but,
       being a little man, he could not see him for the
       crowd.'*
       Father God, forgive us for being what we are,
       obstructions to the view of those who look for
       Christ; make us instead what You would have us
       be; living invitations into the joy of His
       presence: Amen.

226   *' . . . the Son of Man has come to seek and save
       what is lost.'*
       Lord Jesus, You came to look for the lost and
       live with the rejected; breathe into us Your love
       and compassion that we may live as You lived,
       and set Your joy in heaven above our comfort
       on earth: Amen.

       *Also to be found at Third Sunday after Trinity, second year
       (195)*

MATTHEW 25.1–13   Nineteenth Sunday after
                      Trinity

227   *'There were ten girls, who took their lamps and
       went out to meet the bridegroom.'*
       Lord, whose Son will come again in glory, send
       us hope, hope for the future bringing present
       power; hope which looks beyond all human help;
       hope in Christ, our present Saviour and our
       future Judge: Amen.

228 *'But at midnight a cry was heard: "Here is the
bridegroom!"'*
Lord, may the vision of Your future coming shape
our present lives, that we may pray today and
work today in joyful expectation of tomorrow,
ready at all times for our King and Judge: Amen.

*Also to be found at Twenty seventh Sunday after Trinity,
first year (121)*

MATTHEW 7.13–20   Twentieth Sunday after Trinity

229 *' . . . the gate that leads to life is small, and the
road is narrow . . . '*
Lord, take our scattered thoughts and feelings
and align them with Your will; that the
confinement of the narrow way may be our
freedom and our delight, and we may live now in
the largeness of eternal life: Amen.

230 *'Beware of false prophets . . . '*
Lord God, You have made us able to tell good
from evil; give us grace always to follow the
good, for the sake of our Lord who did Your will
at the cost of His life, and made us free to
follow Him: Amen.

231 ' . . . *the Son of Man is sovereign even over the*
Sabbath.'
Lord, keep our lives simple in a complex world,
and help us to live by the single rule of love, that
all the universe may be reunited with its Maker:
Amen.

Also to be found at Sixth Sunday after Epiphany, first year
(25) and at Trinity Sunday, second year (189)

232 '*There was a man in the congregation who had a*
withered arm . . . '
Lord, Your love shines in a loveless world; shine
on us, Your weak and disabled followers, that we
may be strong to love as You have loved us, and
heal the world at the cost of our lives, for Your
sake: Amen.

Also to be found at Sixth Sunday after Epiphany, first year
(26)

MARK 2.18–22   Twenty Second Sunday after
Trinity

233 '*As long as they have the bridegroom with them,*
there can be no fasting.'
God of the depressed and anxious, pierce the
outer skin of cheerfulness which masks our secret
fears, and fill our inner being with Your joy, the
joy of resurrection and of living with our Lord:
Amen.

Also to be found at Fifth Sunday after Epiphany, first year
(23)

234 '*No one sews a patch of unshrunk cloth on to an
old coat . . .* '
Lord of new beginnings, save us from patching up
our polluted world and continuing in selfish
greed, but make us new people, fit for a new
heaven and a new earth, through Jesus Christ our
Lord, the beginning and end of all things: Amen.

*Also to be found at Fifth Sunday after Epiphany, first year
(24)*

JOHN 3.1–8   Twenty Third Sunday after Trinity

235 '*It is spirit that gives birth to spirit.*'
Lord Jesus, who did all things well, give us the
power to live as You lived, to attract as You
attracted, and to speak as You spoke, that Your
Spirit may come in power and people be born
again into Your kingdom: Amen.

236 '*The wind blows where it wills . . .* '
Lord, You see us harness the world's energy for
our own ends; make us willing to be harnessed by
the energy of Your Spirit, and drive us into the
world new people, living evidence of Your power
and love: Amen.

237 ' . . . *nothing that goes into a man from outside can defile him.*'
Spirit of truth, when evil around us distracts our attention from evil within, show us where true danger lies, and bring us the strength to expose the whole of our lives to Your healing power: Amen.

238 '*For from inside, out of a man's heart, come evil thoughts . . .* '
Lord, save us from fear, fear of the inner depths of the mind; show us the matching depth of Your forgiveness, and fill us with the love which reaches every corner of the universe: Amen.

Also to be found at Sixth Sunday after Trinity, first year (79)

239 ' "*This is the heir*", they said; "*let us kill him.*" '
Lord, You rode straight into the power of the enemy to suffer and die; give us the strength to follow You to the centres of opposition in this world and the confidence which confronts power with love: Amen.

Also to be found at Palm Sunday, first year (45) and at Palm Sunday, second year (167)

240 ' . . . *so they flung him out of the vineyard and
killed him.*'
Lord Jesus, rejected by the religious men of Your
time, help us to accept Your presence in the
modern world, to see You in unexpected people
and in unexpected places; to acknowledge Your
power in our lives and in the lives of others:
Amen.

MARK 13.5–13   Twenty Sixth Sunday after Trinity

241 ' . . . *but the end is still to come.*'
Lord Jesus, who when the solar system ends will
shine brighter than the sun, help us now to make
the light of Your presence known in all the
world, for the sake of Your love: Amen.

Twenty seventh Sunday after Trinity, first year (122)

242 '*You will be flogged in synagogues.*'
Father God, Your Son was tortured and killed on
our account; give us the strength to share that
suffering which turns to joy, and that death which
is swallowed up in resurrection: Amen.

*Also to be found at Fifth Sunday after Easter, second year
(182)*

243　'*Imposters will come claiming to be messiahs or prophets . . .* '
Lord of love, who died on the Cross; Lord of joy, who rose from the dead; Lord of peace, who lives with the Father, send into our modern world prophets who live and speak Your truth: Amen.

244　'*Imposters will come claiming to be messiahs or prophets . . .* '
Lord and judge of our polluted society; save us from putting our trust in economic miracles and social science, but give us love and faithfulness to heal the sick, and feed the hungry, while we wait for Your Son to come and judge the world: Amen.

Saints Days
and other festivals

LUKE 2.15–21   **The Circumcision Of Christ or The Naming Of Jesus (January 1st)**

245   *'Eight days later the time came to circumcise him . . .'*
Lord God, Your Son was circumcised and made one with His people under the law; grant that we may be crucified and made one with our Lord by His grace, that we may live now in the freedom of His resurrection: Amen.

JOHN 1.14–18   **The Epiphany or The Manifestation Of Christ To The Gentiles (January 6th)**

246   *' . . . he came to dwell among us, and we saw his glory . . .'*
Lord Jesus, men brought You token gifts and You gave Your whole self for the life of the world; help us to give You our whole selves, to receive Your grace and truth, and to be in the world lights marking Your presence and reflecting Your glory: Amen.

MATTHEW 19.27–30   **The Conversion Of St Paul (January 25th)**

247   *' . . . anyone who has left brothers or sisters, father, mother or children, land or houses for the sake of my name will be repaid many times over . . .'*
Lord God, keep us faithful to our vision of Your Son, that we may, like Paul, throw everything away for the sake of knowing Christ Jesus our Lord, and, sharing in His sufferings, may know His resurrection: Amen.

LUKE 2.22–35   The Presentation Of Christ In The Temple or The Purification Of St Mary The Virgin (February 2nd)

248   *'Guided by the Spirit he came into the temple . . .'*
Lord God, You kept faith with Simeon and
showed him the infant king; give us grace to put
all our trust in Your promises, and the patience
to wait a lifetime for their fulfilment, through
Jesus Christ, our Lord, on whom faith depends
from start to finish: Amen.

*Also to be found at Second Sunday after Christmas, first
year (13)*

JOHN 15.1–10   St Matthias The Apostle (February 24th)

249   *' . . . every fruiting branch he cleans . . .'*
God of the living, prune from our lives all weak,
diseased and useless growth, and keep our
thoughts and actions rooted in our Lord, that
love and joy may multiply in our lives and in the
world, to Your glory: Amen.

Also to be found at First Sunday after Trinity, first year (69)

LUKE 1.26–38a   The Annunciation Of The Blessed Virgin Mary (March 25th)

250   *' . . . as you have spoken, so be it.'*
God of the impossible, whose angel spoke of
Isaac's birth and Sarah laughed, give to us the
mind of Mary, who heard a greater promise and
believed, that as Your Spirit speaks in our
hearts, so it may be in our lives, through Jesus
Christ, our Lord, obedient to death and King for
ever: Amen.

Also to be found at Fourth Sunday in Advent, first year (8)

MARK 13.5–11   **St Mark The Evangelist**
                               (April 25th)

251   *'But before the end the Gospel must be proclaimed to all nations . . . '*
God of the universe, the sun will swallow up the earth but You will remain; be for us the centre of our lives and swallow up anxiety, that we may radiate Your love and peace in Christ to all the world: Amen.

JOHN 14.1–14   **St Philip and St James, Apostles**
                               (May 1st)

252 *'I am the way . . . '*
God of all knowledge, beyond the reach of those who would stand and wait for proof, help us to do the will of Christ, and to come to know You in Him: Amen.

Also to be found at Fourth Sunday after Easter, second year (180) and at Trinity Sunday, first year (67)

JOHN 15.12–17   **St Barnabas The Apostle**
                               (June 11th)

253 *'You are my friends, if you do what I command you.'*
Lord, help us like Barnabas to lay everything at Your feet and receive the gift of faith, and help us to go like Barnabas to share Your gift with others, that people in today's world may put their trust in You: Amen.

LUKE 1.57–66, 80   **The Nativity Of St John The Baptist (June 24th)**

254   ' . . . *you will be the Lord's forerunner, to prepare his way . . .* '
Lord Jesus, You chose John to go before You and the twelve to follow after; choose again now, that men and women, messengers of God, may serve You in a world gone wrong, and bring Your love to all men: Amen.

MATTHEW 16.13–20   **St Peter The Apostle (June 29th)**

255   ' *"And you,"* he asked, *"who do you say I am?"* '
Lord Jesus, our King and companion, feed our minds with the right question at the right time, that our hearts may expand to know You, and our lives expand to serve You in Your kingdom: Amen.

LUKE 1.39–49   **The Visitation Of The Blessed Virgin Mary (July 2nd)**

256   '*Tell out, my soul, the greatness of the Lord.*'
Lord Jesus, grant us the double joy of Mary and Elizabeth; the joy of carrying You in our hearts and the joy of recognizing You in the hearts of others, that out of joy may come praise, telling out the greatness of God our Saviour: Amen.

JOHN 20.11–18   St Mary Magdalen (July 22nd)

257 *'Jesus said, "Mary!"'*
Risen Lord, when we are blinded by doubt and
despair and do not know where You are, come
to us and call us by name; fill the empty
universe; fill us with joy; turn us into living
evidence that we are forgiven and You are alive
for ever: Amen.

MARK 10.35–45   St James The Apostle (July 25th)

258 *'... to sit at my right or left is not for me to
grant.'*
Lord Jesus, make us, like James, able to follow
You to death not for a place in heaven but
because we have seen You on earth: Amen.

Also to be found at Fifth Sunday in Lent, second year (166)

LUKE 9.28–36   The Transfiguration Of Our Lord
            (August 6th)

259 *'... they saw his glory ...'*
Living Lord, who links us with eternity, grant us
the vision which passes in a flash but lasts for
ever, and grant us all our lives to follow You:
Amen.

*Also to be found at Fourth Sunday in Lent, first year (41)
and at Fourth Sunday in Lent, second year (163)*

LUKE 22.24-30   **St Bartholomew The Apostle (August 24th)**

260   *'Then a jealous dispute broke out . . . '*
Lord, forgive us for our divisions and heal the
wounds we have given and received, that we may
be strong to serve and love our opponents, and
Your greater body the Church may be made
whole: Amen.

MATTHEW 14.1-12   **The Beheading Of St John The Baptist (August 29th)**

261   *'The king . . . had John beheaded in prison.'*
Lord Jesus, You see the end from the beginning;
do not show us the end, because we are afraid,
but be with us now, and give us courage now to
speak out against evil and live dangerously, for
the sake of Your everlasting kingdom: Amen.

LUKE 11.27-28   **The Nativity Of The Blessed Virgin Mary (September 8th)**

262   *' "Happy the womb that carried you . . . " . . .
"No, happy are those who hear the word of God
and keep it".'*
Father God, may the words of Christ direct all we
do, and the mind of Christ direct all we think,
that we may come to know most intimately the
love at the heart of the universe, the love of the
Father for the Son and the Son for the Father:
Amen.

MATTHEW 9.9–13   St Matthew The Apostle (September 21st)

263   *'Jesus saw a man named Matthew at his seat in the custom-house, and said to him, "Follow me" . . . '*
Lord God, whose Son called Matthew on a working day to follow Him, send us Your grace, that we may see and hear our Lord in our weekday lives, and count everything loss for the sake of knowing Him: Amen.

Also to be found at Fourth Sunday after Epiphany, first year (21)

MATTHEW 18.1–6, 10   St Michael And All Angels (September 29th)

264   *'The disciples came to Jesus and asked, "Who is the greatest in the kingdom of Heaven?" '*
Lord and Father, Your Son was a crucified outcast in this world; save us from seeking status in Your sight or in the sight of others, but make us like Him who made Himself nothing to bring us into Your kingdom: Amen.

LUKE 10.1–9   St Luke The Evangelist (October 18th)

265   *'When you come into a town . . . heal the sick there, and say, "The kingdom of God has come close to you".'*
Lord God, who gave to Luke the doctor a new and greater power to heal; extend our limited lives that we may extend Your kingdom, and all men may be whole: Amen.

JOHN 15.18-27 **St Simon And St Jude, Apostles**
(October 28th)

266 '*As they persecuted me, they will persecute you.*'
Lord Jesus, killed by hate and raised by love, help
us to be Your witnesses in a hostile world, to
show most love where there is most hate, and to
live united with one another until You come
again: Amen.

*Also to be found at Seventh Sunday after Trinity, second
year (204)*

MATTHEW 5.1-12 **All Saints (November 1st)**

267 '*How blest are those who know their need of God;
the kingdom of Heaven is theirs.*'
Lord and Father, help us to worship You in
spirit and in truth, and with the fellowship of all
Your family; with those who live in faith in the
modern world, and those who died in faith before
we were born, that together we may worship
You in joy for ever: Amen.

MATTHEW 4.12-20 **St Andrew The Apostle**
(November 30th)

268 '*And at once they left their nets and followed him.*'
Lord God, who sees us busy with our own affairs,
break into our lives with Your disturbing call,
and show us what things to abandon and what
new things to do, for the sake of Him who is
worth the loss of all things: Amen.

*Also to be found at Second Sunday after Epiphany, first
year (18)*

JOHN 20.24–29   **St Thomas The Apostle
(December 21st)**

269 '*He said, "Unless I see . . . I will not believe."* '
Lord Jesus Christ, alive for ever, open our eyes
to see You and our lives to touch Yours, that
with Thomas we may know our Lord and our
God, and be witnesses to others of Your
resurrection: Amen.

LUKE 11.49–51   **St Stephen (December 26th)**

270 '*I will send them prophets and messengers; and
some of these they will persecute and kill.*'
Lord God, You sent the Prince of Peace into a
violent world to be killed; send us into our world
of wealth, hunger and self-regard, that men may
explore the limits of Christ's love as we live and
die for others, in the power of Your Spirit: Amen.
*Also to be found at Twelfth Sunday after Trinity, second
year (213)*

JOHN 21.20–25   **St John The Evangelist
(December 27th)**

271 '*It is this same disciple who attests what has here
been written. It is in fact he who wrote it, and we
know that his testimony is true.*'
God of joy and of our senses, give us understanding minds to grasp the evidence of those
who saw and heard and touched the living Christ,
that we may know Him in our hearts and our
joy may be full: Amen.

272 '*Herod . . . gave orders for the massacre of all
children in Bethlehem . . . of the age of two years
or less . . .*'
Lord and maker of man, the only species which
freely kills its own kind from fear and greed, tear
from our hearts the seeds of violence, and
implant that love for You which is the only
ground of our security: Amen.

Additional collects for
Prayer Book Gospels

273 ' . . . *all the town came out to meet Jesus; and
   when they saw him they begged him to leave the
   district . . .* '
   Lord Jesus, who showed total power over evil and
   was asked to go away, we surrender to the power
   of love and ask You to stay, that Your love may
   conquer our concern for self and safety, and lead
   us into Your Kingdom: Amen.

MATTHEW 13.24–30

274 '*Let them both grow together till harvest . . .* '
   Lord of this world, where good and bad flourish
   together and cannot be pulled apart, fix our wills
   on growing in Your Spirit so that evil may not
   stifle us, but we grow to produce love, joy and
   peace in Your eternal Kingdom: Amen.

275 '*Let them both grow together till harvest . . .* '
   Lord of light, who alone can resolve the greys of
   this world into black and white, keep us from
   judging other people, and make us fit for Your
   Kingdom: Amen.

276 '*A Canaanite woman . . . came crying out, "Sir!*
   have pity . . . My daughter is tormented . . ." '
   Lord, when those we love are attacked by evil,
   help us never to give up the search for grace and
   healing, but to spend our lives following You and
   trusting in Your love and power: Amen.

277 '*It is not right to take the children's bread and*
   throw it to the dogs.'
   Lord of all men, sent to Your own people but
   exposed to pressures from strangers, help us when
   we face demands which lie beyond our limits;
   grant the vision which sees the expanding task,
   and the strength which is able to carry it out; to
   the glory of Your name: Amen.

278 '*Woman, what faith you have!*'
   Lord, You found faith in unexpected people, in
   people scorned by the religious men of your
   time; help us to live in Your Church so close to
   those outside it that we may know and share
   true faith across the border: Amen.

279 *'Why do you look at the speck of sawdust in your brother's eye . . . ?'*
Lord of all perfection, who did not criticize the sick but made them well, strengthen our desire to be like You, and make us perfect in our love for others: Amen.

LUKE 16.1–9

280 *'There was a rich man who had a steward, and . . . this man was squandering the property.'*
Lord of the world which modern industry has ravaged, grant us not new resources but a new concern, to leave the search for finer methods of plunder, and look for harmony with You and with the world: Amen.

LUKE 19.41–47

281 *'When he came in sight of the city, he wept over it . . .'*
Lord, who loved the proud and the violent, send us Your Spirit, that we may be like You and take the road You took in the world You died for: Amen.

282 '*Set your mind on God's kingdom . . .*'
Loving Father, Your Son refused all the
kingdoms of the world for our sake; teach us
how to be poor for His sake, that we may serve
Him with an undivided mind and love Him with
all our heart, in the joy of Your kingdom: Amen.

LUKE 7.11–17

283 '*The dead man sat up and began to talk . . .*'
Living Lord, attend the funeral of Your Church,
and touch our coffin of self-preserving zeal to
bring us back to life, life lived for others, life
eternal lived for You, our Saviour: Amen.

284 '*God has shown his care for his people.*'
Lord, who raised to life the dead son of a widow,
grant us such care for other people's needs that
Your power may work through us to bring new
life to the dead, now and for ever: Amen.

LUKE 14.1–11

285 ' *. . . go and sit down in the lowest place . . .* '
Lord of modern society, guide us to our true
place in it: help us to serve rather than compete,
to redeem rather than condemn, to remove
injustice rather than condone, and to live
wherever You direct, sharing the joy of the
kingdom: Amen.

286 *'How do you come to be here without your*
   wedding clothes?'
   Lord, send Your love into our hearts to set our
   wills on fire, that we may do the work You have
   given us to do, and, clothed in Your character,
   be fit for Your kingdom: Amen.

JOHN 4.46–54

287 *'He . . . begged him to go down and cure his son*
   . . . Then Jesus said, "Return home, your son will
   live".'
   Lord, who gave a father faith and gave a sick boy
   life, grant us faith and life together, that we may
   live now in the freedom of Your resurrection:
   Amen.

JOHN 6.5–14

288 *'Collect the pieces left over, so that nothing may be*
   lost.'
   Lord, come to our throw-away society and give
   us a greater care for Your gifts, that the
   resources of Your earth may be used for the
   needs of Your family, and all may have enough:
   Amen.

COLLECTS FOR PRAYER BOOK GOSPELS - INDEX

GENERAL INDEX OF PASSAGES

By the author's husband:

Godthoughts
Dick Williams

'A devotional happening for the young-minded' – prayers and meditations very much in the modern idiom by one of the authors of *The Gospel in Scouse*. More than 25,000 copies already sold in the UK.

Godfacts
Dick Williams

Dick Williams, writing in the same style as in *Godthoughts*, explores the facts of the Creed. Every statement of the Creed describes a belief in reality. It 'sums up what has followed in man's thinking through the ages once he has chosen to believe in Christ'.
This form of expression will appeal to those still thinking their way through Christianity, as well as those using it in private or group readings.

Prayers for Today's Church
edited by Dick Williams

'A collection of prayers which reflect the aspirations and preoccupations of our present age. Edwyn Young contributes a prayer for entertainers, Dick Williams for drop-outs, Christopher Idle for space travel, Andrew Warner for immigrants.
'It is a book of common prayer in that it expresses our common concern for God's world – and in that respect at least it deserves to stand alongside the book of Common Prayer.'
From an introduction by the Bishop of Liverpool.

Other Falcon books include:

Ministry in the Seventies
Clive Porthouse (editor)

A group of leading evangelicals set out their thoughts on the future of the Church and its ministry. They succeed in combining foresight and strategy with practical suggestions at 'ground level'.

Family Worship

This book contains an order of service for Family Worship, a selection of prayers, New and Old Testament pointed psalms, and metrical psalms, canticles and songs in the *Youth Praise* idiom. Only available direct from CPAS. Inspection copy available on request.

Teaching the Families
Michael Botting

This handbook is designed to bring fresh ideas to those preparing and speaking at family services. It contains introductions to the use of visual aids – soundstrips, overhead projectors, drama and puppetry. These are linked to 60 talk outlines covering the Christian year, the Christian life, and some biblical characters.

Into the World
the needs and limits of Christian involvement
J. N. D. Anderson

A lucid and comprehensive introduction to the subject of Christian involvement in the world. Abortion, euthanasia, social justice, politics, international relations, the arts, are a few of the many topics studied.

My God is real
David Watson

Exceptionally well reviewed, this readable book sets out the basics of the gospel as understood by one of Britain's outstanding young preachers.

Jesus is alive
Kairos Group

Experimental ways of presenting the gospel on the basis of words – dramatized readings, modern parables, dialogues. A valuable source book for youth groups, women's meetings and church services.

The Facts of the Matter
Ian Barclay

Ian Barclay presents some basic Christian beliefs in his own lively style with many colourful literary illustrations.

He is everything to me
Ian Barclay

This author's second book is in a similar style to his already popular *The Facts of the Matter* but on a very different subject. Here is a modern devotional exposition of Psalm 23 all will find helpful.

Other Falcon booklets include:

Task unfinished
prayers for mission
Michael Saward

In this selection of 50 prayers for mission, the topics range from conversion, disheartened missionaries, the pioneer missionary and evangelists, to unemployment, the mass-media, revolution and space exploration.

Faith
Robert Crossley

A reasoned examination of what we mean by faith, and how it applies to such issues as faith in God, faith and good works, justification by faith, and living by faith.

Hope
Robert Crossley

Christian hope is firmly grounded in scriptural truth. The author contrasts this with some false hopes held by people.

God in Control
Peter Coombs

Peter Coombs firmly asserts that God is still in control amid such a man-dominated society. Having created the world He has not abandoned us. We see how He guides us today in all aspects of our existence in a world which is not as capricious as we might believe.